THE MARKET SQUARE DOG

James Herriot

Illustrated by Ruth Brown

St. Martin's Press
New York

On market days when the farmers around Darrowby brought their goods to the little town to sell, I used to take a walk across the cobbled square to meet the farmers who gathered there to chat. One of the farmers was telling me about his sick cow when we saw the little dog among the market stalls. The thing that made us notice the dog was that he was sitting up, begging, in front of the stall selling cakes and biscuits.

'Look at that little chap,' the farmer said. 'I wonder where he's come from?'

As he spoke, the stallholder threw him a bun which the dog
devoured eagerly, but when the man came round and
stretched out a hand the little animal trotted away. He stopped,
however, at another stall which sold eggs, butter, cheese and
scones. Without hesitation, he sat up again in the begging
position, rock steady, paws dangling, head pointing expectantly.

I nudged my companion. 'There he goes again.
I always think a dog looks very appealing sitting up like that.'

The farmer nodded. 'Yes, he's a bonny little thing, isn't he?
What breed would you call him?'

'A cross, I'd say. He's like a small sheepdog, but there's a
touch of something else – maybe terrier.'

It wasn't long before the dog was munching a biscuit, and this time I walked over to him, and as I drew near I spoke gently. 'Here, boy,' I said, squatting down in front of him. 'Come on, let's have a look at you.'

He turned to face me, and for a moment two friendly brown eyes gazed at me from a wonderfully attractive face. The fringed tail waved in response to my words, but as I moved nearer he turned and trotted away among the market-day crowd until he was lost to sight.

I was standing there, trying to see where he had gone, when a young policeman came up to me.

'I've been watching that wee dog begging among the stalls all morning,' he said, 'but, like you, I haven't been able to get near him.'

'Yes, it's strange. You can see he's friendly, but he's also afraid. I wonder who owns him.'

'I reckon he's a stray, Mr Herriot. I'm interested in dogs myself and I fancy I know just about all of them around here. But this one is a stranger to me.'

I nodded. 'I'm sure you're right. Anything could have happened to him. He could have been ill-treated by somebody and run away, or he could have been dumped from a car.'

'Yes,' the policeman replied, 'there are some cruel people about. I don't know how anybody can leave a helpless animal to fend for itself like that. I've had a few tries at catching him, but it's no good.'

The memory stayed with me for the rest of the day. It is our duty to look after the animals who depend on us and it worried me to think of the little creature wandering about in a strange place, sitting up and asking for help in the only way he knew.

Market day is on a Monday and on the Friday of that week my wife Helen and I had a treat planned for ourselves; we were going to the races in Brawton. Helen was making up a picnic basket with home-made ham-and-egg-pie, chicken sandwiches and a chocolate cake. I was wearing my best suit and I couldn't help feeling very smart because country vets have to work mostly in the fields and cowsheds and I hardly ever got dressed up. Helen, too, had put on her best dress and a fancy hat I had never seen before. As a vet's wife, she too had to work very hard and we weren't able to go out together very often.

We were just about to leave the house when the doorbell rang. It was the young policeman I had been talking to on market day.

'I've got that dog, Mr Herriot,' he said. 'You know – the one that was begging in the market square.'

'Oh good,' I replied, 'so you managed to catch him at last.'

The policeman paused. 'No, not really. One of our men found him lying by the roadside about a mile out of town and brought him in. I'm afraid he's been knocked down. We've got him here in the car.'

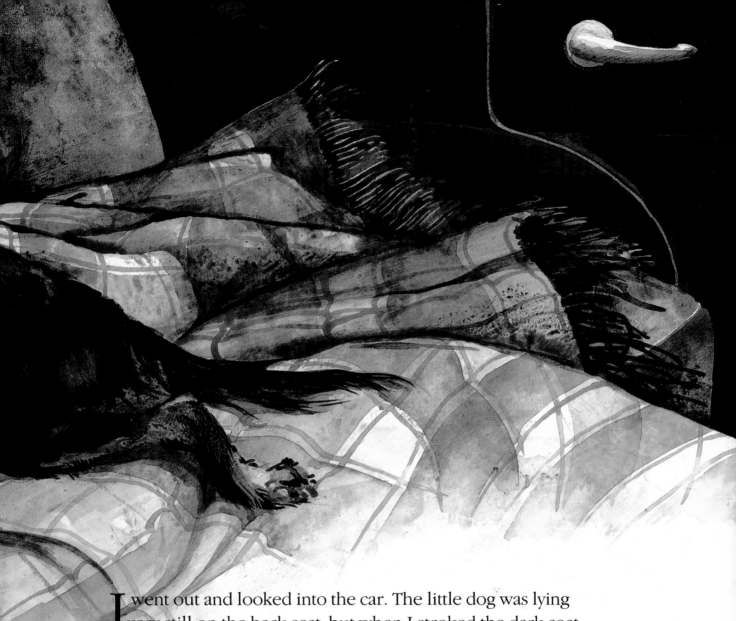

I went out and looked into the car. The little dog was lying very still on the back seat, but when I stroked the dark coat his tail stirred briefly.

'He can still manage a wag, anyway,' I said.

The policeman nodded. 'Yes, there's no doubt he's a good-natured wee thing.'

I tried to examine him as much as possible without touching because I didn't want to hurt him, but I could see that he had cuts all over his body and one hind leg lay in such a way that I knew it must be broken. When I gently lifted his head, I saw that one eyelid was badly torn so that the eye was completely closed. But the other soft brown eye looked at me trustingly.

'Can you do anything for him, Mr Herriot?' asked the policeman. 'Can you save him?'

'I'll do my best,' I replied.

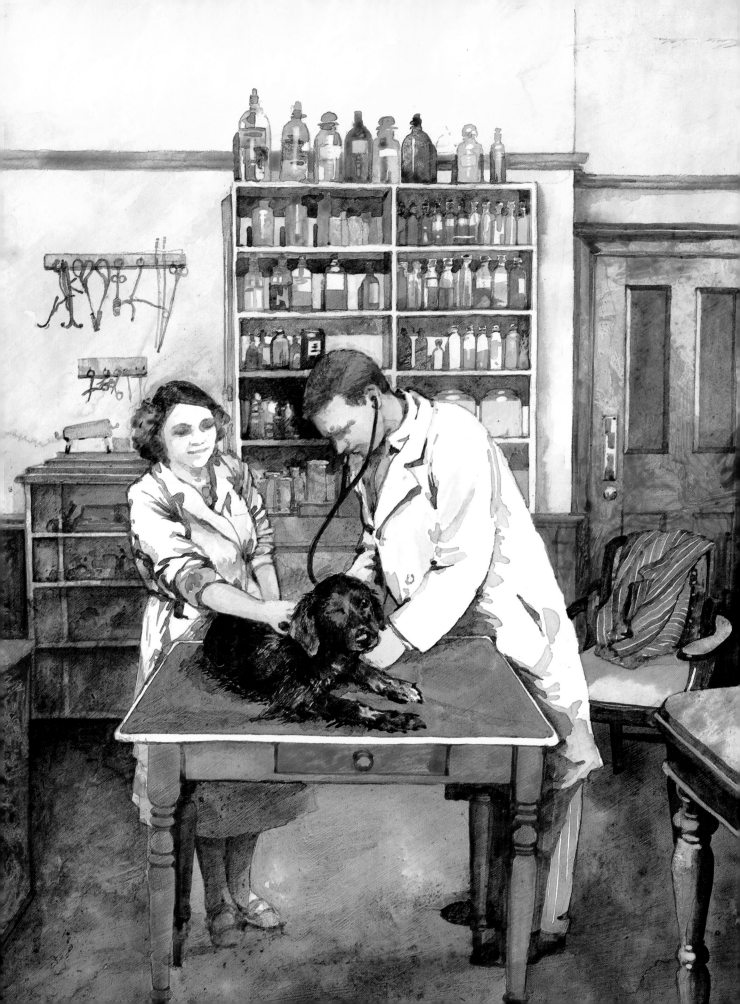

I carried the little animal into the surgery and laid him on the table.

'There's an hour or two's work here, Helen,' I said to my wife. 'I'm very sorry, but we won't be able to go to the races.'

'Never mind,' she replied. 'We must do what we can for this fellow.'

Rather sadly she took off her fancy hat and I took off my good jacket. Dressed in our white coats we began to work.

Helen was used to helping me and she gave the anaesthetic, then I set the broken leg in plaster and stitched up the wounds. The worst thing was the eye because even after I had stitched the eyelid it was still bruised and tightly closed and I was worried that he might lose the sight in that eye.

By the time we had finished, it was too late to go out anywhere, but Helen was quite cheerful. 'We can still have our picnic,' she said.

We carried the sleeping dog out to the garden and laid him on a mat on the lawn so that we could watch him as he came round from the anaesthetic.

Out there in the old high-walled garden the sun shone down on the flowers and the apple trees. Helen put on her fancy hat again and I put my smart jacket back on and as we sat there, enjoying the good things from the picnic basket, we felt that we were still having a day out. But Helen kept glancing anxiously at the little dog and I knew she was thinking the same thing as I was. Would he be all right after all that we had done for him and, even then, what was going to happen to him? Would his owners ever come to claim him, because if they didn't, he had nobody in the world to look after him.

Since he had been found by the police, he was officially classified as a stray and had to go into the kennels at the police station. When I visited him there two days later, he greeted me excitedly, balancing well on his plastered leg, his tail swishing. All his fear seemed to have gone. I was delighted to see that the injured eye was now fully open, and the swelling down.

The young policeman was as pleased as I was. 'Look at that!' he exclaimed. 'He's nearly as good as new again.'

'Yes,' I said, 'he's done wonderfully well.' I hesitated for a moment. 'Has anybody enquired about him?'

He shook his head. 'Nothing yet, but we'll keep hoping, and in the meantime we'll take good care of him here.'

I visited the kennels often, and each time the shaggy little creature jumped up to greet me, laughing into my face, mouth open, eyes shining. But nobody seemed to want him.

After a few more days it was clear that no owner was going to claim him, and my only hope was that somebody else would take him and give him a home.

There were other stray dogs in the kennels, and on one visit I saw a farmer calling to collect his wandering sheepdog.

Then a family was overjoyed at being reunited with their handsome golden retriever.

Finally a little old lady came in and tearfully gathered her tiny Yorkshire terrier into her arms. But nobody came for my little patient.

Various strangers came too, looking for a pet, but nobody seemed to be interested in him. Maybe it was because he was only a mongrel and the people who visited the kennels wanted a more elegant dog – yet I knew that he would make a perfect pet for anybody.

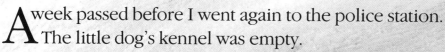

A week passed before I went again to the police station. The little dog's kennel was empty.

'What's happened?' I asked the policeman. 'Has somebody taken him?'

The policeman looked very grave. 'No,' he replied, 'I'm afraid he's been arrested.'

'Arrested?' I said in astonishment. 'What do you mean?'

'Well,' he said, 'it seems that it's against the law for a dog to go begging in the market square so he has been taken into police custody.'

I was bewildered. 'What are you talking about? A dog can't be arrested.'

The policeman, still very solemn, shrugged his shoulders. 'This dog was.'

'I still don't know what this is all about,' I said. 'Where is he now?'

'I'll take you to him,' the policeman replied.

We left the police station and walked a short way along the road to a pretty cottage.

We went inside and there, in the sitting-room, curled up in a big new doggy bed was my little friend. Two small girls were sitting by his side, stroking his coat.

The policeman threw back his head and laughed. 'I've just been kidding you, Mr Herriot. This is my house and I've taken him as a pet for my two daughters. They've been wanting a dog for some time and I've got so fond of this wee chap that I thought he'd be just right for them.'

A wave of relief swept over me. 'Well, that's wonderful,' I said and I looked at his kind face gratefully. 'What's your name?' I asked.

'Phelps,' he replied. 'PC Phelps. And they call me Funny Phelps at the police station because I like playing jokes on people.'

'Well, you certainly took me in,' I said. 'Arrested indeed!'

He laughed again. 'Well, you've got to admit he's in the hands of the law now!'

I laughed too. I didn't mind having the joke played on me because, funny Phelps or not, he was obviously a nice Phelps and would be a kind master for my doggy friend.

It was a happy day when I took the plaster off the little dog's leg and found that the break had healed perfectly. All the nasty cuts had healed, too, and when I lifted him down from the table, the small girls held up a beautiful new red collar with a lead to match. Their new pet liked the look of them because he sat up in that position I remembered so well, his paws dangling, his face looking up eagerly. The begging dog had found a home at last.